Beginning Programming Using Retro Computing

Learn BASIC with a Commodore Emulator

Gerald Friedland

Apress®

Beginning Programming Using Retro Computing: Learn BASIC with a Commodore Emulator

Gerald Friedland
Berkeley, CA, USA

ISBN-13 (pbk): 978-1-4842-4145-5   ISBN-13 (electronic): 978-1-4842-4146-2
https://doi.org/10.1007/978-1-4842-4146-2

Library of Congress Control Number: 2018965497

Managing Director, Apress Media LLC: Welmoed Spahr
Acquisitions Editor: Aaron Black
Development Editor: James Markham
Coordinating Editor: Jessica Vakili

Cover image designed by Freepik (www.freepik.com)

Distributed to the book trade worldwide by Springer Science+Business Media New York, 233 Spring Street, 6th Floor, New York, NY 10013. Phone 1-800-SPRINGER, fax (201) 348-4505, e-mail orders-ny@springer-sbm.com, or visit www.springeronline.com. Apress Media, LLC is a California LLC and the sole member (owner) is Springer Science + Business Media Finance Inc (SSBM Finance Inc). SSBM Finance Inc is a **Delaware** corporation.

For information on translations, please e-mail rights@apress.com, or visit www.apress.com/rights-permissions.

Apress titles may be purchased in bulk for academic, corporate, or promotional use. eBook versions and licenses are also available for most titles. For more information, reference our Print and eBook Bulk Sales web page at www.apress.com/bulk-sales.

Any source code or other supplementary material referenced by the author in this book is available to readers on GitHub via the book's product page, located at www.apress.com/978-1-4842-4145-5. For more detailed information, please visit www.apress.com/source-code.

Printed on acid-free paper

Table of Contents

TABLE OF CONTENTS

About the Author

Gerald Friedland started programming with the Commodore 16 at the age of 7. Ever since then his life has been dominated by bits and teaching how to juggle them to others. Today, Gerald has a PhD in computer science and teaches introductory programming and data science classes as adjunct professor at the University of California, Berkeley. Apart from a research career as a computer and data scientist, with two books and a list of publications in multimedia and machine learning conferences and journals, he is also an active contributor in the maker community. His company, Audeme, produces an offline speech recognition shield for Arduino boards.

About the Technical Reviewer

Massimo Nardone has a master of science degree in computing science from the University of Salerno, Italy, and has more than 24 years of experience in the areas of security, web/mobile development, cloud, and IT architecture. His IT passions are security and Android.

Specifically, he has worked as a project manager, software engineer, research engineer, chief security architect, information security manager, PCI/SCADA auditor, and senior lead IT security/cloud/SCADA architect.

He has also worked as a visiting lecturer and supervisor for exercises at the Networking Laboratory of the Helsinki University of Technology (Aalto University), and he holds four international patents (in the PKI, SIP, SAML, and proxy areas).

He currently works as the chief information security officer (CISO) for Cargotec Oyj and is a member of the ISACA Finland Chapter board.

Massimo has reviewed more than 45 IT books for different publishing companies and is the coauthor of *Pro JPA 2 in Java EE 8* (Apress, 2018), *Beginning EJB in Java EE 8* (Apress, 2018), and *Pro Android Games* (Apress, 2015).

Acknowledgments

I would like to say a big thank-you to the people in the various Commodore Facebook groups who encouraged me with in-depth comments on the first draft of this book. Without their help and encouragement, this book would not be publicly available. If you like what you see in this book, please make a point of joining one or more of the following groups: *Commodore 16/Plus/4*, *Commodore 64/128*, and *Commodore PET, VIC-20,16, Plus/4,64,128*. Interact with super-nice people like Petri Stenberg, Trevor, Mattias Olli, Patrick Bakker, Anders Persson, Chris Snowden, and others. A special thanks goes to Marti Hoogterp for doing an amazing early review of the book.

I would also like to thank the staff at Apress, most notably Aaron Black, Jessica Vakili, and James Markham.

I also need to thank my daughter, Mona, for using the book and giving me suggestions. Finally, this book would not have been possible without my mother buying a Commodore 16 from Aldi in Germany in 1986. Thank you, mum!

Preface

I created this book as a birthday present to my 7-year-old daughter. It introduced programming to her using an emulation of the Commodore 16/Plus 4 system. The system's BASIC 3.5 is an effective programming system that was used to teach hundreds of thousands of children in the 1980s, the so-called 8-bit generation. The educational principle of these computers and this book is that children at that age are fascinated to see that words they write have the power to do things like play sounds, draw graphics, or do their math homework. BASIC 3.5 is a simple programming system that minimizes distraction, and therefore the parental interaction needed, while maximizing feedback and therefore the learning progress for the child.

I taught myself programming with a Commodore 16 computer at very young age. When my daughter finally turned 7, about the age when I started, I wanted her to start to learn programming as well. I researched the market for elementary school programming tools and could not find anything that I liked. None of the modern tools I found were "turn on and program" like the 8-bit Commodore computers. Furthermore, many teaching portals are online, and having to expose my elementary school child to the Internet caused me anxiety. In contrast, once the emulator is in full-screen mode, the learner is immersed in this environment without distraction.

Following this concept, this book was written to be understandable with the reading and math skills of a child in second grade. The only exceptions are this preface containing setup instructions and the appendix.

Chapter 1 and the following chapters assume that a Commodore 16/116, Plus 4, or 128 is ready to go. The appendix describes several ways of setting up such a system in today's technical infrastructure and also how to load and save programs. The latter was left out of the main part of the book because of its complexity and the potential for damage (e.g., overwriting of files).

Whether you want your kid to follow the same path as my daughter or you'd love to catch up on what you missed in the 1980s or you are interested in learning fundamental programming concepts with a system that has passed the test of time, this book intends to make the basics of programming so easy that an elementary school child can self-study with it. From there, the transition to a modern, more complex programming language, like Python, is much easier.

Enjoy!

Setting Up

This book contains examples that can be run with Commodore BASIC 3.5. This version of BASIC was originally available on the Commodore 16, Plus 4, and 116. The examples in this book will also work on the Commodore 128, which came with BASIC 7.0. The popular Commodore 64 came with BASIC 2.0, which lacks most of the graphic and sound functionality and cannot be used with this book. The appendix contains more details on how to set up your Commodore BASIC 3.5 experience. There are essentially two ways to time warp back into the 1980s: using an emulator or re-activating the original hardware. This appendix will outline both of them.

Using an Emulator

Whatever emulation option you choose, you will most likely want the original Commodore keyboard. The easiest way to get a Commodore keyboard feeling is to use a modern keyboard with stickers. They are, among other locations, available here: http://www.4keyboard.com.

While there are small differences between Commodore keyboards, the Commodore 64 version of the stickers will work. The following image shows the arrangement of the Commodore stickers on a modern keyboard that was used for this book:

At the time of writing this book, several emulators are usable without any software installation. For example, a browser-based Commodore 128 emulator is available at `https://vice.janicek.co/c128/`.

The aforementioned online emulator is based on VICE, which is the most popular Commodore emulator. VICE is developed as open source and is available at `http://vice-emu.sourceforge.net/`.

VICE can be used offline on any PC or Mac and even on your Android cell phone. The part of the emulator used to write this book is called *xplus4*.

To get close to the full experience, I recommend you install VICE on a dedicated computer, for example, on a Raspberry PI. The following images show a Raspberry Pi with a casing and a controller, available at various locations:

More information on how to build a Raspberry PI dedicated to Commodore emulation can be found at the home page of the Retro Pie project: `https://retropie.org.uk/`.

While Retro Pie installs VICE, by default the GUI makes only the Commodore 64 emulator visible. To enable BASIC 3.5, the Commodore Plus 4 emulation needs to be used. There are two ways of doing that.

- Start the Plus 4 emulation directly from a command line using this command:

    `/opt/retropie/emulators/vice/bin/xplus4`

- Start the emulator from a GUI, after enabling the Plus 4 emulation in the file `es_systems.cfg`. The file is an XML configuration file and how to edit it is described here:

    `https://github.com/RetroPie/RetroPie-Setup/wiki/EmulationStation`

The entry for the Commodore Plus 4 system should look like this:

```
<system>
  <name>c16</name>
  <fullname>Commodore Plus4</fullname>
  <path>/home/pi/RetroPie/roms/c16</path>
  <extension>.crt .d64 .g64 .prg .t64 .tap .x64 .zip .vsf .CRT .D64 .G64
  .PRG .T64 .TAP .X64 .ZIP .VSF</extension>
  <command>/opt/retropie/supplementary/runcommand/runcommand.sh 0 _SYS_ c16
  %ROM%</command>
  <platform>c16</platform>
  <theme>c16</theme>
</system>
```

At the time of writing this book, the process is also described in detail on Ian Hill's web site at `https://ianwilliamhill.co.uk/c16rp/`.

Re-activating the Original Hardware

Re-activating an original Commodore computer is by far the most nostalgic experience. There are only two drawbacks to this approach. First, the original computers connect to an analog TV either using an NTSC or PAL signal, so their resolution and update frequency do not meet today's ergonomic standards for eye comfort. Also, with most modern TVs not supporting analog signals anymore, an adapter is needed. The typical way to connect a Commodore computer to a modern TV is to use the S-Video signal that is available on most Commodore computers. The second drawback is that loading and saving programs took a long time in the 1980s. I definitely recommend connecting a floppy disk unit, for example, the Commodore 1541, which works with the Commodore 16/116, Plus 4, C64, and Commodore 128. Tape recorders will literally take minutes to even load a small program. A limited amount of hard disks were available at the time.

Fortunately, there is a seemingly ever-growing community of people connecting modern storage and interfaces (such as USB) to Commodore 8-bit computers. For example, commercial outlets for hardware adapters that serve this purpose include the following:

```
http://www.commodore16.com/commodore16-com-shop/
https://gglabs.us/
http://store.go4retro.com/
```

Unfortunately, describing the process of re-activating the original hardware for the various Commodore systems, modern hardware options, and different screen combinations could easily fill another book. I therefore recommend checking with local retro computing user groups, web sites, and forums, including the following:

```
https://cbm8bit.com/
https://www.instructables.com/howto/commodore/
https://hackaday.com/?s=commodore
```

CHAPTER 1

The Start Screen

At this point, I will assume you are set up and see the following screen. If not, ask a parent to follow the instructions in the preface.

```
COMMODORE BASIC V3.5 60671 BYTES FREE
3-PLUS-1 ON KEY F1

READY.
■
```

Congratulations! You are ready to go!

Whenever you start a new chapter in this book, make sure you start at this screen. This screen is called the *startup screen*.

One more thing: Do you see the blinking rectangle? This rectangle is called the *cursor*. The cursor is where everything happens. Always pay attention to where the cursor is.

With that, let's move on to the next chapter.

© Gerald Friedland 2019
G. Friedland, *Beginning Programming Using Retro Computing*,
https://doi.org/10.1007/978-1-4842-4146-2_1

Summary

Each chapter will have a short summary of what you have learned. In this chapter, you learned about the start screen and the cursor.

CHAPTER 2

Simple Drawing

In this chapter, you will get to know your keyboard. You can use it to move the cursor, type letters and numbers, and even draw.

Knowing Your Keyboard

Look at your keyboard. Do you see the symbols above the letters?

You access the *right* symbols by pressing the SHIFT key SHIFT and the letter key at the same time.

© Gerald Friedland 2019
G. Friedland, *Beginning Programming Using Retro Computing*,
https://doi.org/10.1007/978-1-4842-4146-2_2

You access the *left* symbols by pressing the  key and the letter key at the same time. This odd key is called the Commodore key.

Let's try a couple of simple examples.

Press **SHIFT** and **A**.

What do you see? You should see this symbol: ♣.

Now press **RETURN** and try this:

1. Press **Commodore** and **A**.

2. Press **Commodore** and **S**.

3. Press **SHIFT** and **RETURN**.

4. Press **Commodore** and **Q**.

5. Press **Commodore** and **W**.

6. Press **SHIFT** and **RETURN**.

7. Press **Commodore** and **Z**.

8. Press **Commodore** and **X**.

The result should look like this:

The drawing looks like a window! Try drawing other things this way!

You can also use the arrow keys to move the cursor up and down. They look like this:

The next pages have examples of more drawings. They were made by Mona, a 7-year-old girl. You can try to copy them on your screen. But even better, experiment and draw your own pictures.

A Snake

Check out this snake:

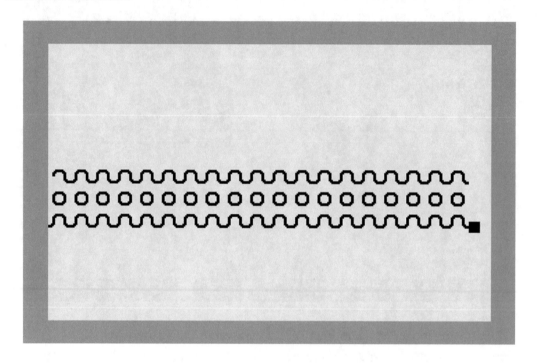

Note   You can press RETURN many times to clear the screen. The CLR/HOME key brings the cursor back into the upper corner.

A Playing Card

Try to make this playing card:

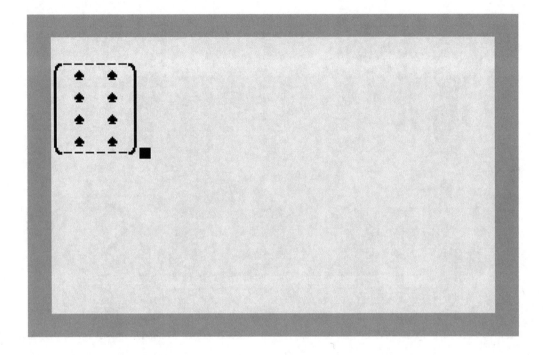

An Island

Check out this island:

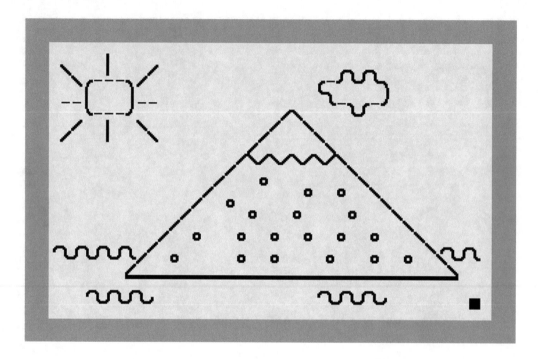

Summary

In this chapter, you practiced using the keyboard. For drawings, you can use SHIFT or the Commodore key together with another key.

CHAPTER 3

Math

In this chapter, you will do math using the computer.

Start from the beginning with this screen again:

© Gerald Friedland 2019
G. Friedland, *Beginning Programming Using Retro Computing*,
https://doi.org/10.1007/978-1-4842-4146-2_3

Remember, the black blinking rectangle is called the *cursor*.

Now let's do some math. Type the following:

PRINT 3-2

Press **RETURN**.

What do you see?

You see that the computer gave the answer: 1.

Let's try another one.

Type the following:

PRINT 2*5

Press **RETURN**.

What do you see?

```
COMMODORE BASIC V3.5 60671 BYTES FREE
3-PLUS-1 ON KEY F1
READY.
PRINT 3-2
 1

READY.
PRINT 2*5
 10

READY.
■
```

The symbol * is read as "times." So, the computer saw "2 times 5." The computer is right: 2 times 5 (or 2*5) is 10!

So, you did subtraction and multiplication.

What other math can you do? The symbol + means "plus," the symbol - means "minus," the symbol * means "times," and the symbol / means "divide by."

Try it!

Summary

The computer can solve math sentences when you start them with PRINT.

CHAPTER 4

Sound

The computer can make sounds. Let's try that! Make sure you have some speakers connected and turned on. Let's start the Commodore 16 again.

© Gerald Friedland 2019
G. Friedland, *Beginning Programming Using Retro Computing,*
https://doi.org/10.1007/978-1-4842-4146-2_4

Now you need to tell the computer how loud it should be. The command is as follows:

VOL 8

Press **RETURN**.

8 is the loudest, 1 is the quietest, and 0 means no sound.

It looks like this:

Then, let's actually play a sound. The command is SOUND. Try it by typing this:

SOUND 1,266,50

Press **RETURN**.

It looks like this:

```
COMMODORE BASIC V3.5 60671 BYTES FREE
3-PLUS-1 ON KEY F1

READY.
VOL 8

READY.
SOUND 1,266,50

READY.
■
```

15

What happens? If you did not hear anything, check your speakers.

Now try typing this:

SOUND 1,266,200

Press **RETURN**.

It looks like this:

```
COMMODORE BASIC V3.5 60671 BYTES FREE
3-PLUS-1 ON KEY F1

READY.
VOL 8

READY.
SOUND 1,266,50

READY.
SOUND 1,266,200

READY.
```

What happened? Do you know why?

The last number is how long the sound is played.

Now try typing this:

SOUND 1,666,200

Press **RETURN**.

It looks like this:

```
COMMODORE BASIC V3.5 60671 BYTES FREE
3-PLUS-1 ON KEY F1
READY.
VOL 8
READY.
SOUND 1,266,50
READY.
SOUND 1,266,200
READY.
SOUND 1,666,200
READY.
■
```

What happened? Do you know why?

The middle number is the tone pitch. Try this:

SOUND 1,100,200

Press **RETURN**.

Then type this:

SOUND 1,200,200

Press **RETURN**.

Then type this:

SOUND 1,400,200

Press **RETURN**.

Finally, type this:

SOUND 1,800,200

Press **RETURN**.

See how the tone changes?

One more thing. Computers can also fart!

Type this:

SOUND 3,266,10

Press **RETURN**.

Did you hear the computer fart?

If you make the first number a **3**, you get *noise* instead of a *tone*.

Try it: How can you change the length of the noise? How can you change the pitch of the noise?

Summary

In this chapter you learned the VOL and SOUND commands and experimented with sounds of different lengths and types.

CHAPTER 5

Colors

Let's add **some** color!

You just have to press the Commodore key and a number key at the same time.

Remember, the Commodore key looks like this:

The number keys look like this:

Do you see the BLK, WHT, RED, CYI? These are short versions of the words for the colors *black*, *white*, *red*, and *cyan* (a bright blue). So, if you press the Commodore key and a number together, the cursor will change into this color.

© Gerald Friedland 2019
G. Friedland, *Beginning Programming Using Retro Computing*,
https://doi.org/10.1007/978-1-4842-4146-2_5

Press **Commodore** and **3** together and then type **MONA**.

It looks like this:

```
COMMODORE BASIC V3.5 60671 BYTES FREE
3-PLUS-1 ON KEY F1

READY.
MONA█
```

Now you can draw in color. Try it!

Also try other colors by pressing the Commodore key and another number.

Another way to change colors is with the COLOR command.

Type this:

COLOR 0,6

Press **RETURN**.

It should look like this:

```
COMMODORE BASIC V3.5 60671 BYTES FREE
3-PLUS-1 ON KEY F1

READY.
COLOR 0,6

READY.
```

Now type this:

COLOR 4,6

Press **RETURN**.

It should look like this:

```
COMMODORE BASIC V3.5 60671 BYTES FREE
3-PLUS-1 ON KEY F1

READY.
COLOR 0,6

READY.
COLOR 4,6

READY.
```

Found the trick?

The COLOR command takes two numbers. The first number is the part of the screen you want to change: 0 specifies the background, 1 specifies the letters, and 4 specifies the border. Then, the colors are numbered just like the letters on the keyboard.

> 1 = black, 2 = white, 3 = red, 4 = cyan, 5 = purple, 6 = green,
> 7 = blue, 8 = yellow, 9 = orange, 10 = brown, 11 = yellow/greenish,
> 12 = pink, 13 = blue-greenish, 14 = light blue, 15 = dark blue,
> and 16 = light green.

Now try to set the background to light blue and the border to yellow!

It should look like this:

```
    COMMODORE BASIC V3.5 60671 BYTES FREE
    3-PLUS-1 ON KEY F1
READY.
COLOR 0,6
READY.
COLOR 4,6
READY.
COLOR 0,14
READY.
COLOR 4,8
READY.
■
```

Summary

In this chapter, you learned key combinations to change the color, and you used the COLOR command.

CHAPTER 6

Graphics

So far, you have drawn by hand. Now you will let the computer draw!

Type this:

GRAPHIC 2,1

Press **RETURN**.

The result looks like this:

READY.

© Gerald Friedland 2019
G. Friedland, *Beginning Programming Using Retro Computing*,
https://doi.org/10.1007/978-1-4842-4146-2_6

You have switched the computer into the graphics mode.

Now, you can type this:

BOX 1,0,0,100,100

Press **RETURN**.

Take a look at the result:

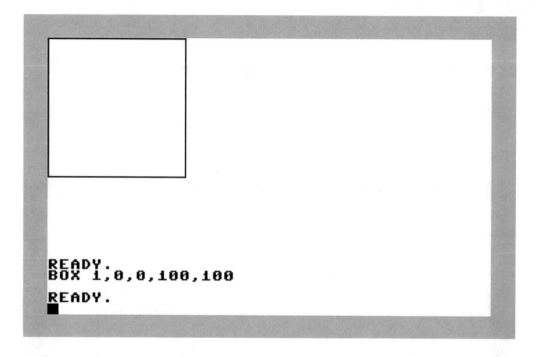

```
READY.
BOX 1,0,0,100,100

READY.
```

A box! But the command BOX takes so many numbers!

How does this work?

Let's take a look again. The command was as follows:

BOX 1,0,0,100,100

The first number of BOX is 1. A 1 means draw in black, and a 0 means draw in white.

The second number is 0. This number tells the computer how far to the right the upper-left corner of the box should be. 0 means all the way to the left, and 320 is all the way to the right.

The third number is also 0. This number tells the computer how far to the bottom the upper-left corner of the box should be. 0 means all the way up, and 160 is all the way to the bottom.

The fourth number is 100. This number tells the computer how far to the right the lower-right corner of the box should be. 0 means all the way to the left, 320 is all the way to the right, and 100 is somewhere in between.

The fifth number is 100. This number tells the computer how far to the bottom the lower-right corner of the box should be. 0 means all the way up, 160 is all the way to the bottom, and 100 is somewhere in between.

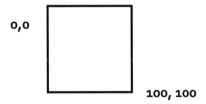

Complicated? Let's play with it!

Try this:

BOX 1,101,0,201,100

Press **RETURN**.

Look at the result shown here:

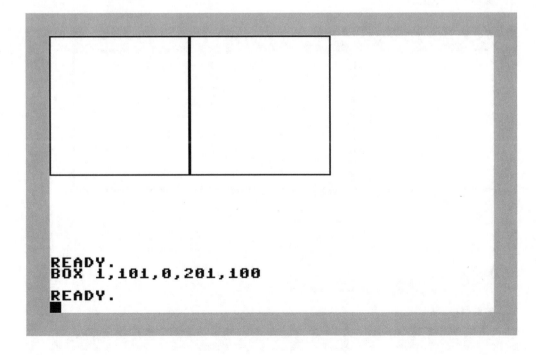

This command added a second box next to the first one.

What are the numbers?

The first number is 1 again, for drawing in black.

The second number is 101. Remember the third number of the first box was 100? The third number of the first box was how far right the bottom corner of the first box is. You want to start your new box just right of that, so you add 1, as in 100+1=101.

The third number is 0 again, just like in the first box. This is so that the upper-left corner of the second box starts at the same height as the first one.

The fourth number is 201. The fourth number indicates how far to the right the lower-right corner of the box should be. Well, the first box ended at 100. You want the second box to have the same size. So, you add 100 to the start of the second box, which is 101. 100+101=201.

The fifth number is 100 again because you want the lower-right corner of the box to be at the same height level as the lower-right corner of the first box.

Let's try one more:

BOX 1,202,0,302,100

Press **RETURN**.

Look at the result:

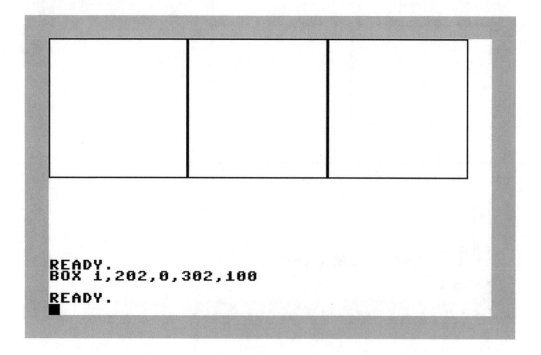

```
READY.
BOX 1,202,0,302,100

READY.
```

Can you explain it?

Let's try one last one:

BOX 1,0,101,302,150

Press **RETURN**.

Look at the result and explain it!

Here is the result:

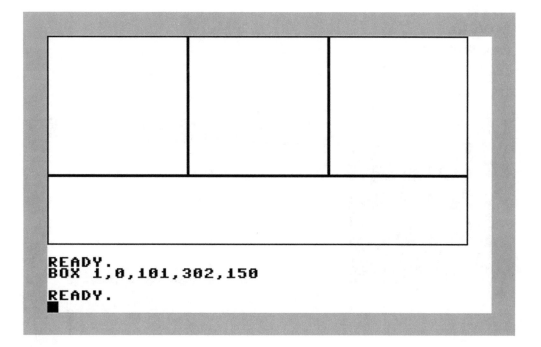

```
READY.
BOX 1,0,101,302,150

READY.
```

There are many other graphics commands that do cool things. It would take many pages to explain them, so it's best if you experiment with them on your own. You will need basic addition and subtraction. The first number always indicates draw in black (1) or draw in white (0). Draw in white can be used to erase. The second number always indicates how far to the right. The third number always indicates how far to the bottom. Try another command.

Type this:

PAINT 1,1,1

Press **RETURN**.

The PAINT command colors a structure.

This is the result:

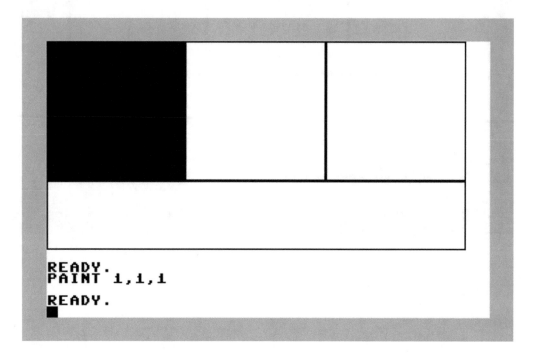

Let's fill the third rectangle.

Type this:

PAINT 1,203,1

Press **RETURN**.

This is the result:

Can you fill the other rectangles too?

There's one more command to play with!

Type this:

CIRCLE 1, 150, 125, 150, 25

Press **RETURN**.

What is the result?

Summary

You learned that the computer can draw boxes and circles automatically. Numbers tell the computer the position on the screen.

CHAPTER 7

Errors

This chapter explains something less fun than what you've been doing so far. It talks about "errors." You will see errors at the most unexpected times. They will appear to slow you down. They can be frustrating too. But they are only here to help you.

Errors are the way the computer tells you it does not understand something. When you see an error, it is best to take a deep breath. Then compare what you see in this book against what you did. Sometimes you may have to start from the beginning of a chapter again. It happens to all of us.

There are many types of errors. The following two are the most frequent.

A *syntax error* is an error that tells you that you spelled a command incorrectly. See the mistake in the following screen?

```
COMMODORE BASIC V3.5 60671 BYTES FREE
3-PLUS-1 ON KEY F1

READY.
PLINT 3-2

?SYNTAX ERROR
READY.
```

© Gerald Friedland 2019
G. Friedland, *Beginning Programming Using Retro Computing*,
https://doi.org/10.1007/978-1-4842-4146-2_7

Yes, PLINT is wrong. It is PRINT. When you correct the spelling, the command will work without error. See the next screen:

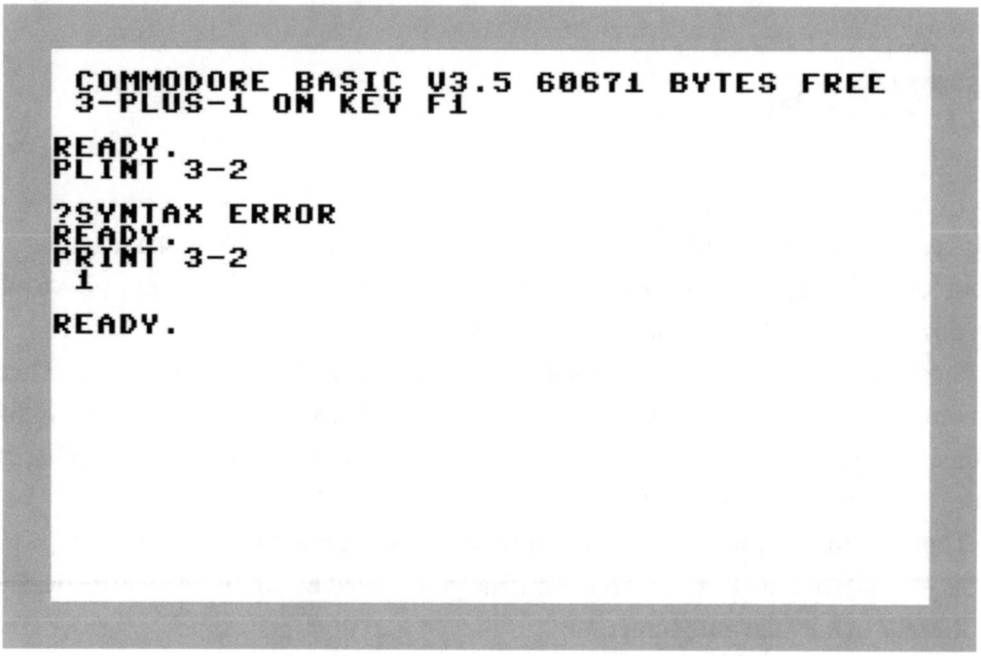

```
COMMODORE BASIC V3.5 60671 BYTES FREE
3-PLUS-1 ON KEY F1

READY.
PLINT 3-2

?SYNTAX ERROR
READY.
PRINT 3-2
 1

READY.
```

Another type of error is an *illegal quantity* error. It might sound complicated. Here is an example:

```
COMMODORE BASIC V3.5 60671 BYTES FREE
3-PLUS-1 ON KEY F1

READY.
COLOR 0,200

?ILLEGAL QUANTITY ERROR
READY.
```

This error tells you that a number is wrong. In this case, COLOR cannot take 200. When the command is corrected with the right number, it will work, as shown in the next screen:

```
COMMODORE BASIC V3.5 60671 BYTES FREE
3-PLUS-1 ON KEY F1
READY.
COLOR 0,200
?ILLEGAL QUANTITY ERROR
READY.
COLOR 0,12
READY.
```

As explained earlier, when you see an error, carefully read the command again. Programming is hard, and sometimes finding errors can take some time. Even programmers with many years of experience have to deal with them.

Summary

Errors are there to make us think. You can learn from them.

CHAPTER 8

Variables

This chapter talks about how to make the computer remember things. For this chapter, please start fresh (turn the computer off and on or restart).

The computer memory works with *variables*. Variables save a message or a number so that you can use it later.

Try this:

AGE=7 (press **RETURN**)

PRINT AGE (press **RETURN**)

```
COMMODORE BASIC V3.5 60671 BYTES FREE
3-PLUS-1 ON KEY F1

READY.
AGE=7

READY.
PRINT AGE
  7

READY.
█
```

© Gerald Friedland 2019
G. Friedland, *Beginning Programming Using Retro Computing*,
https://doi.org/10.1007/978-1-4842-4146-2_8

What happened?

AGE was set to 7. Then you printed AGE. The result is 7.

What if you set AGE=25 and print it?

Here is the result:

```
COMMODORE BASIC V3.5 60671 BYTES FREE
3-PLUS-1 ON KEY F1

READY.
AGE=7

READY.
PRINT AGE
 7

READY.
AGE=25

READY.
PRINT AGE
 25

READY.
■
```

Variables can do more than numbers. They can also store messages.

Type this:

MSG$="HELLO, MONA" (press **RETURN**)

PRINT MSG$ (press **RETURN**)

The result looks like this:

```
COMMODORE BASIC V3.5 60671 BYTES FREE
3-PLUS-1 ON KEY F1

READY.
MSG$="HELLO,MONA"

READY.
PRINT MSG$
HELLO,MONA

READY.
■
```

Just like with numbers, PRINT returns what is stored in the variable. You can do it again and again!

Type:

PRINT MSG$ (press **RETURN**)

PRINT MSG$ (press **RETURN**)

PRINT MSG$ (press **RETURN**)

The result looks like this:

```
COMMODORE BASIC V3.5 60671 BYTES FREE
3-PLUS-1 ON KEY F1

READY.
MSG$="HELLO,MONA"

READY.
PRINT MSG$
HELLO,MONA

READY.
PRINT MSG$
HELLO,MONA

READY.
PRINT MSG$
HELLO,MONA

READY.
PRINT MSG$
HELLO,MONA

READY.
```

You have to store the variable only once, and you can reuse it—until you turn off the computer or close the Commodore program.

Be careful, though. For messages, you need to add $ to the variable name. Otherwise, the computer complains with an error!

For example, type this:

MSG="HELLO, MONA"

Press **RETURN**.

This will result in an error, as shown here:

```
READY.
MSG$="HELLO,MONA"

READY.
PRINT MSG$
HELLO,MONA

READY.
PRINT MSG$
HELLO,MONA

READY.
PRINT MSG$
HELLO,MONA

READY.
PRINT MSG$
HELLO,MONA

READY.
MSG="HELLO, MONA"

?TYPE MISMATCH ERROR
READY.
```

Remember, numbers can have any name. Messages need to have a name with $ at the end. The message itself needs to be in quote marks. It is easy to forget the second quote!

Summary

You have learned how to store numbers and messages in variables.

CHAPTER 9

Math and Variables

Can you do math with variables? Yes, you can!

Try this:

AGE=6 (press **RETURN**)

PRINT AGE+1 (press **RETURN**)

```
   3-PLUS-1 ON KEY F1
READY.
AGE=7

READY.
PRINT AGE
 7

READY.
AGE=25

READY.
PRINT AGE
 25

READY.
AGE=6

READY.
PRINT AGE+1
 7

READY.
```

© Gerald Friedland 2019
G. Friedland, *Beginning Programming Using Retro Computing*,
https://doi.org/10.1007/978-1-4842-4146-2_9

What happened?

The result is 7 because AGE is 6 and 6+1=7.

What happens when you try this:

PRINT AGE+2 (press **RETURN**)

PRINT AGE+3 (press **RETURN**)

AGE stays 6, and 6+2=8 and 6+3=9. No surprise here.

You can check that AGE is still 6 by typing this:

PRINT AGE

Press **RETURN**.

Here is the result:

```
READY.
PRINT AGE
 25

READY.
AGE=6

READY.
PRINT AGE+1
 7

READY.
PRINT AGE+2
 8

READY.
PRINT AGE+3
 9

READY.
PRINT AGE
 6

READY.
```

AGE never changed.

Now try this:

AGE=AGE+1 (press **RETURN**)

PRINT AGE (press **RETURN**)

See this screen for the result:

```
READY.
PRINT AGE+1
 7

READY.
PRINT AGE+2
 8

READY.
PRINT AGE+3
 9

READY.
PRINT AGE
 6

READY.
AGE=AGE+1

READY.
PRINT AGE
 7

READY.
█
```

What happened?

Using the = command, AGE was set to AGE+1.

So, AGE is 6. That means AGE+1 is 6+1=7. Using =, you set AGE to 6+1. So, you set AGE to 7. That's why the result printed is 7.

Let's try a different example. Type this:

APPLE=5 (press **RETURN**)

BANANA=2 (press **RETURN**)

FRUITS=APPLE+BANANA (press **RETURN**)

PRINT FRUITS (press **RETURN**)

```
PRINT AGE
 6

READY.
AGE=AGE+1

READY.
PRINT AGE
 7

READY.
APPLE=5

READY.
BANANA=2

READY.
FRUITS=APPLE+BANANA

READY.
PRINT FRUITS
 7

READY.
```

What happened? Well, APPLE is 5. BANANA is 2. FRUITS is then set to APPLE+BANANA or 5+2. And you know that 5+2=7. Therefore, FRUITS is 7.

Now let's add pears to the fruits.

PEAR=3 (press **RETURN**)

FRUITS=FRUITS+PEAR (press **RETURN**)

PRINT FRUITS (press **RETURN**)

What do you think the result is?

```
APPLE=5

READY.
BANANA=2

READY.
FRUITS=APPLE+BANANA

READY.
PRINT FRUITS
 7

READY.
PEAR=3

READY.
FRUITS=FRUITS+PEAR

READY.
PRINT FRUITS
 10

READY.
```

What happened? PEAR was set to 3. Then FRUITS was set to the number that FRUITS stores (7) plus the number that PEAR stores (3). So, 7+3=10. This is the same as setting FRUITS to APPLE+BANANA+PEAR (5+2+3=10).

Let's check:

```
FRUITS=APPLE+BANANA
READY.
PRINT FRUITS
 7

READY.
PEAR=3

READY.
FRUITS=FRUITS+PEAR

READY.
PRINT FRUITS
 10

READY.
FRUITS=APPLE+BANANA+PEAR

READY.
PRINT FRUITS
 10

READY.
```

Yay! See what else you can do with variables. Try also +, -, * and /.

Note   Choose your variable names so that the first two letters don't overlap. BANANA and BARBEQUE are the same variable because the both start with BA. BANANA and BBQ are fine (BA and BB). Also, variable names cannot start with a number or be a command. For example, PRINT=1 will give an error.

Summary

You can use variables to store the result of math. You can also use variables in a math sentence.

CHAPTER 10

A Program

In this chapter, you will understand what a program is and even write your first one. As usual, start with this screen:

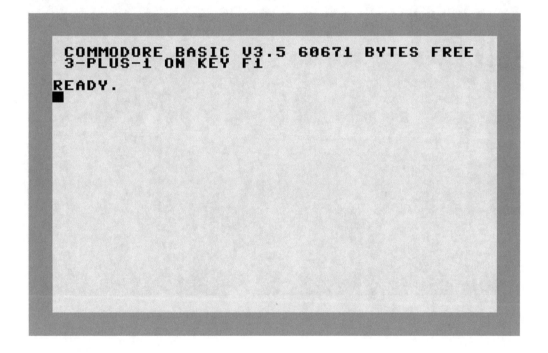

© Gerald Friedland 2019
G. Friedland, *Beginning Programming Using Retro Computing*,
https://doi.org/10.1007/978-1-4842-4146-2_10

Remember, the black blinking rectangle is called the *cursor*.

Let's type a program. It begins with line numbers. Type this:

10 PRINT "HELLO MONA"

Press **RETURN**.

Then type this:

20 GOTO 10

Press **RETURN**.

The screen looks like this:

```
COMMODORE BASIC V3.5 60671 BYTES FREE
3-PLUS-1 ON KEY F1

READY.
10 PRINT "HELLO MONA"
20 GOTO 10
```

Then type this:

RUN

Press **RETURN**.

What happens?

Congratulations! You just ran your first program.

Now press **RUN/STOP ESC** to stop it.

It looks like this:

Type **LIST** and press **RETURN** to see your program again.
It looks like this:

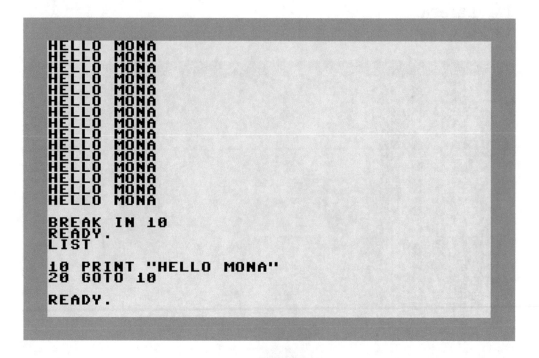

```
HELLO MONA
HELLO MONA
HELLO MONA
HELLO MONA
HELLO MONA
HELLO MONA
HELLO MONA
HELLO MONA
HELLO MONA
HELLO MONA
HELLO MONA
HELLO MONA
HELLO MONA
HELLO MONA

BREAK IN 10
READY.
LIST

10 PRINT "HELLO MONA"
20 GOTO 10

READY.
```

You can now use the arrow keys to move the cursor and
change the program.

Press **UP** four times to go to line 10. Then press **RIGHT** 16 times to put the cursor in front of **MONA**. The *M* is now blinking.

It looks like this:

```
HELLO MONA
HELLO MONA
HELLO MONA
HELLO MONA
HELLO MONA
HELLO MONA
HELLO MONA
HELLO MONA
HELLO MONA
HELLO MONA
HELLO MONA
HELLO MONA
HELLO MONA
HELLO MONA

BREAK IN 10
READY.
LIST

10 PRINT "HELLO MONA"
20 GOTO 10

READY.
```

Now type this:

PAPA

Press **RETURN**.

The 2 is now blinking.

It looks like this:

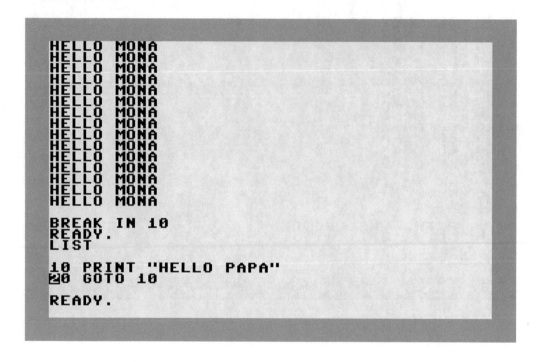

Now press the **DOWN** arrow three times. The cursor is blinking under READY.
It looks like this:

```
HELLO MONA
HELLO MONA
HELLO MONA
HELLO MONA
HELLO MONA
HELLO MONA
HELLO MONA
HELLO MONA
HELLO MONA
HELLO MONA
HELLO MONA
HELLO MONA
HELLO MONA
HELLO MONA
HELLO MONA

BREAK IN 10
READY.
LIST

10 PRINT "HELLO PAPA"
20 GOTO 10

READY.
■
```

Now type **RUN** again.

Press **RETURN**.

What happens?

This!

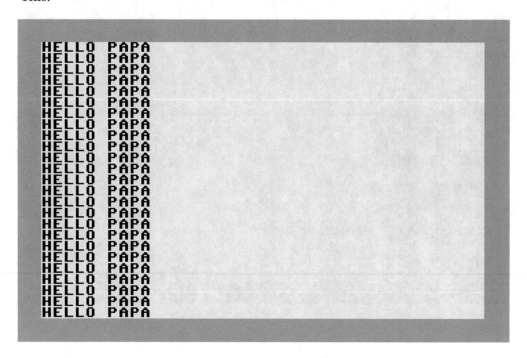

Congratulations! You ran your second program.

You can stop it the same way by pressing **RUN STOP/ESC.**

Try more things by repeating the steps from the earlier pages.

Type **LIST** to see your program.

Use the arrow keys, and type new letters to change the program.

Press **RETURN** to enter it into the computer.

Go below READY, and type RUN and press **RETURN** to start it again.

If you want to write a new program, type **NEW** and then press **RETURN**.

Chapter 14 contains many examples of programs to play with.

Summary

So, what is a program? A program is like a cooking recipe. It is a list of commands. You can run a program over and over again after typing it in only once.

CHAPTER 11

Questions

Can computers ask questions in a program? Yes.

In a program, the computer can ask questions and store the answer in a variable. The command for that is INPUT. INPUT also needs a variable name. For example, typing **INPUT AGE** will ask for a number and store the number in the variable AGE.

Make sure you are at the startup screen. Type the following program:

10 PRINT "HOW OLD IS MONA"; (press **RETURN**)

20 INPUT AGE (press **RETURN**)

30 PRINT "MONA IS"; (press **RETURN**)

40 PRINT AGE; (press **RETURN**)

50 PRINT "YEARS OLD." (press **RETURN**)

Usually, the computer jumps to the next line after a PRINT command. The semicolon (;) makes the computer stay on the same line.

© Gerald Friedland 2019
G. Friedland, *Beginning Programming Using Retro Computing*,
https://doi.org/10.1007/978-1-4842-4146-2_11

The program looks like this on the computer:

```
READY.
LIST

10 PRINT "HOW OLD IS MONA";
20 INPUT AGE
30 PRINT "MONA IS";
40 PRINT AGE;
50 PRINT "YEARS OLD."

READY.
```

Type **RUN** and press **RETURN** to start the program. The computer will ask for Mona's age. You can type in any number and press **RETURN**. After that, the computer will show you that it saved the number.

It should look like this:

```
READY.
LIST

10 PRINT "HOW OLD IS MONA";
20 INPUT AGE
30 PRINT "MONA IS";
40 PRINT AGE;
50 PRINT "YEARS OLD."

READY.
RUN
HOW OLD IS MONA? 7
MONA IS 7 YEARS OLD.

READY.
■
```

Try **RUN** and press **RETURN** again. Now enter a different number. See how the output changes?

What happened? The INPUT command in line 20 asks for a number and stores it as variable AGE. After you enter a number, lines 30, 40, and 50 piece together the final output sentence. Of course, line 40 is the one outputting the number.

Let's try another example. Type this:

10 PRINT "HOW MANY APPLES"; (press **RETURN**)

20 INPUT APPLE (press **RETURN**)

30 PRINT "HOW MANY BANANAS"; (press **RETURN**)

40 INPUT BANANA (press **RETURN**)

50 FRUITS=APPLE+BANANA (press **RETURN**)

60 PRINT "WE HAVE"; (press **RETURN**)

70 PRINT FRUITS; (press **RETURN**)

80 PRINT "FRUITS." (press **RETURN**)

```
COMMODORE BASIC V3.5 60671 BYTES FREE
3-PLUS-1 ON KEY F1

READY.
10 PRINT"HOW MANY APPLES";
20 INPUT APPLE
30 PRINT"HOW MANY BANANAS";
40 INPUT BANANA
50 FRUITS=APPLE+BANANA
60 PRINT"WE HAVE";
70 PRINT FRUITS;
80 PRINT"FRUITS.";
```

Type **RUN** and press **RETURN** to start the program. The computer will ask how many apples (lines 10 and 20). You can type in any number and press **RETURN**. After that, the computer will ask how many bananas (lines 30 and 40). You can type in any number and press **RETURN**. Then, the computer will add the numbers in APPLE and BANANA into the variable FRUITS (line 50). It will then output the result in a sentence (lines 60, 70, and 80). Take a look:

```
COMMODORE BASIC V3.5 60671 BYTES FREE
3-PLUS-1 ON KEY F1

READY.
10 PRINT"HOW MANY APPLES";
20 INPUT APPLE
30 PRINT"HOW MANY BANANAS";
40 INPUT BANANA
50 FRUITS=APPLE+BANANA
60 PRINT"WE HAVE";
70 PRINT FRUITS;
80 PRINT"FRUITS.";
RUN
HOW MANY APPLES? 5
HOW MANY BANANAS? 2
WE HAVE 7 FRUITS.
READY.
```

Is this familiar?

Can you add pears to the program? Hint: You can add lines 45 and 46, and you need to change line 50.

Summary

The INPUT command allows you to ask question to the user. The response is stored in a variable.

61

CHAPTER 12

Counting

It's time you give the computer a lot more work! For example, let's make the computer count for you. This chapter introduces FOR and NEXT.

Make sure you are at the startup screen. Type the following:

10 FOR I=1 TO 10 (press **RETURN**)

20 PRINT I (press **RETURN**)

30 NEXT I (press **RETURN**)

Type **RUN** and press **RETURN** to start the program.

```
COMMODORE BASIC V3.5 60671 BYTES FREE
3-PLUS-1 ON KEY F1

READY.
10 FOR I=1 TO 10
20 PRINT I
30 NEXT I
RUN
1
2
3
4
5
6
7
8
9
10

READY.
■
```

© Gerald Friedland 2019
G. Friedland, *Beginning Programming Using Retro Computing*,
https://doi.org/10.1007/978-1-4842-4146-2_12

How does this work?

Line 10 says this:

FOR I=1 TO 10

The variable called I is set to 1 with I=1. So, I=1. Let's skip the other stuff for now.

Line 20 says this:

PRINT I

Well, that just means print the number stored in I. You have done that many times before, for example when you used PRINT AGE.

Line 30 then says this:

NEXT I

The NEXT command exactly does what you think it does. It basically says, "Next number, please!" The computer sets the next number for I. What is the next number? Good question! Remember we skipped some stuff in line 10? Well, let's go back.

FOR I=1 TO 10

While I starts off as 1 with I=1, the line also says 1 TO 10. So, it's like having ten people in a restaurant with the numbers 1 to 10. The next number after 1 is therefore 2. You then go to line 20 to print I again, which now is 2. Then you go to line 30 again, where it says, "Next I, please!" This makes I=3 and returns you to line 10. The game goes on and on and on until you have served all people in the restaurant...ahem...until I=10. Once I is 10, the "Next I, please!" in line 30 will find out that there is no next and therefore will not jump back to line 10 anymore. Let's check this. Type this:

40 PRINT"DONE" (press **RETURN**)

Type **RUN** and press **RETURN** to start the program. You should see this:

```
4
5
6
7
8
9
10

READY.
40 PRINT"DONE"
RUN
1
2
3
4
5
6
7
8
9
10
DONE

READY.
```

That's exactly what you should expect. The computer counts to 10 and then prints DONE because NEXT I finds it is finished.

The entire program looks like this now:

```
READY.
40 PRINT"DONE"
RUN
 1
 2
 3
 4
 5
 6
 7
 8
 9
 10
DONE

READY.
LIST

10 FOR I=1 TO 10
20 PRINT I
30 NEXT I
40 PRINT"DONE"

READY.
```

How would you change the program to count to 100?

Type this:

10 FOR I=1 TO 100 (press **RETURN**)

Type **RUN** and press **RETURN** to start the program. You will see it counting to 100 and then saying DONE.

Here is one more example of really complicated math—something where you really need a computer because it would take way too long to do it by hand. Let's add all the numbers from 1 to 100!

Type this program:

10 SUM=0 (press **RETURN**)

20 FOR I=1 TO 100 (press **RETURN**)

30 SUM=SUM+I (press **RETURN**)

40 NEXT I (press **RETURN**)

50 PRINT "1+2+3+...+100="; (press **RETURN**)

60 PRINT SUM (press **RETURN**)

```
READY.
LIST

10 SUM=0
20 FOR I=1 TO 100
30 SUM=SUM+I
40 NEXT I
50 PRINT"1+2+3+...+100=";
60 PRINT SUM

READY.
RUN
```

Type **RUN** and press **RETURN** to start the program.

What's the answer?

How would you change the program to sum the numbers 1 to 200?

How would you change the program to multiply all numbers from 1 to 10?

Summary

You learned to use FOR and NEXT. These two commands can save you an immense amount of work.

CHAPTER 13

What If?

Sometimes you want to check things. For example, you might want to check a response to a question. This chapter shows how.

As usual, make sure you are at the startup screen. Type the following program:

10 PRINT"HOW OLD IS MONA"; (press **RETURN**)

20 INPUT AGE (press **RETURN**)

30 IF AGE<7 THEN PRINT"TOO LOW" (press **RETURN**)

40 IF AGE>7 THEN PRINT"TOO HIGH" (press **RETURN**)

50 IF AGE=7 THEN PRINT"CORRECT" (press **RETURN**)

Type **RUN** and press **RETURN** to start the program. The program will ask for Mona's age (lines 10 and 20). You can then enter any number. If the number is smaller than 7, it will say TOO LOW (line 30). If the number is greater than 7, it will say TOO HIGH (line 40), and if the number is exactly 7, it will say CORRECT (line 50).

© Gerald Friedland 2019
G. Friedland, *Beginning Programming Using Retro Computing*,
https://doi.org/10.1007/978-1-4842-4146-2_13

It all looks like this:

```
LIST
10 PRINT"HOW OLD IS MONA";
20 INPUT AGE
30 IF AGE<7 THEN PRINT"TOO LOW":GOTO 10
40 IF AGE>7 THEN PRINT"TOO HIGH":GOTO 10
50 IF AGE=7 THEN PRINT"CORRECT"

READY.
RUN
HOW OLD IS MONA? 6
TOO LOW
HOW OLD IS MONA? 8
TOO HIGH
HOW OLD IS MONA? 7
CORRECT

READY.
```

The command that makes that happen is called IF THEN, and it almost works like human language.

Between IF and THEN is a *condition*. The conditions checks if a variable is smaller than (<), equal to (=), greater than (>),smaller than or equal to (<=), or greater than or equal to (>=) another number or variable.

After THEN is a command that will be executed if the condition is true. If you need more than one command after THEN, you can separate them with colon (:). For example, if you want to have the person try guessing Mona's age again without having to say RUN, you can change lines 30 and 40.

Type this:

30 IF AGE<7 THEN PRINT"TOO LOW":GOTO 10 (press **RETURN**)

40 IF AGE>7 THEN PRINT"TOO HIGH":GOTO 10 (press **RETURN**)

The command GOTO is really just a misspelled "go to". We already used it in Chapter 10. It will jump to the line number given. That is, GOTO 10 will jump to line 10.

Type **RUN** and press **RETURN** to start the program. The program now looks like this:

```
COMMODORE BASIC V3.5 60671 BYTES FREE
3-PLUS-1 ON KEY F1

READY.
10 PRINT"HOW OLD IS MONA";
20 INPUT AGE
30 IF AGE<7 THEN PRINT"TOO LOW"
40 IF AGE>7 THEN PRINT"TOO HIGH"
50 IF AGE=7 THEN PRINT"CORRECT"
RUN
HOW OLD IS MONA? 2
TOO LOW

READY.
RUN
HOW OLD IS MONA? 8
TOO HIGH

READY.
RUN
HOW OLD IS MONA? 7
CORRECT

READY.
■
```

Summary

You learned about IF THEN. Using IF THEN and GOTO together is a powerful combination.

CHAPTER 14

More Programs

This chapter presents programs to type in and play around with. Sometimes you will not know a command. This is not a problem. Often you just need to run the program to see what the command does. Other times you need to experiment to try to understand what the command does. You can experiment by changing the program. For example, leave the command out and see how the program behaves then. You really cannot break anything. Also, there are no wrong solutions. Have fun!

The programs A Song, Boxes, and Circles are special. They are taken from the original Commodore 16 user manual. The programs Piano and Blinking Graphics are similar to programs that appeared in the original Commodore 16 user manual. The manual came out in 1984. It is therefore not an exaggeration to call them *historic programs*!

Make sure you are at the startup screen. Then type in the following programs and start them with **RUN** and press **RETURN**. If you need to stop, press the **ESC/RUN STOP** key (in the upper-right corner). You *never* have to type in the **READY.** part.

© Gerald Friedland 2019
G. Friedland, *Beginning Programming Using Retro Computing,*
https://doi.org/10.1007/978-1-4842-4146-2_14

Animated Hello

Type in the following program, start it with **RUN**, and press **RETURN**. To stop, press the **ESC/RUN STOP** key (in the upper-right corner).

```
10 SCNCLR
20 PRINT"HELLO"
30 FOR I=1 TO 500
40 NEXT I
50 SCNCLR
60 PRINT"MONA"
70 FOR I=1 TO 500
80 NEXT I
90 GOTO 10

READY.
RUN■
```

Note   The command SCNCLR clears the screen. The empty FOR commands in line 30 and 70 serve as delays.

Ball Animation

Make sure you are at the startup screen. Type in the following program, start it with **RUN**, and press **RETURN**. To stop, press the **ESC/RUN STOP** key (in the upper-right corner).

```
10 SCNCLR
20 FOR I=1 TO 400
30 PRINT" ";
40 PRINT"●";
50 FOR J=1 TO 20
60 NEXT J
70 PRINT "▌▌";
80 NEXT I

READY.
RUN█
```

Tip   Press the LEFT arrow key to get the symbol in the PRINT command in line 70.

Playing with Pitch

Make sure you are at the startup screen. Type in the following program, start it with **RUN**, and press **RETURN**. To stop, enter **0**.

```
10 VOL 8
20 PRINT"A NUMBER BETWEEN 1 AND 1015"
25 PRINT "OR 0 FOR END";
30 INPUT X
35 IF X>1015 THEN GOTO 20
40 IF X<0     THEN GOTO 20
50 IF X=0     THEN END
60 SOUND 1,X,10
70 GOTO 20

READY.
RUN
```

Pitch Ladder

Make sure you are at the startup screen. Type in the following program, start it with **RUN**, and press **RETURN**. To stop, press the **ESC/RUN STOP** key (in the upper-right corner).

```
COMMODORE BASIC V3.5 60671 BYTES FREE
3-PLUS-1 ON KEY F1

READY.
10 VOL 7
20 FOR I=0 TO 1015 STEP 5
30 SOUND 1,I,5
40 NEXT I

RUN█
```

Note   The STEP command in line 20 tells FOR to count in steps of five. In other words, instead of counting 0, 1, 2, 3, 4, 5, ..., it is counting 0, 5, 10, 15, 20, 25, and so on.

A Song

Make sure you are at the startup screen. Type in the following program, start it with **RUN**, and press **RETURN**. To stop, press the **ESC/RUN STOP** key (in the upper-right corner).

```
COMMODORE BASIC V3.5 60671 BYTES FREE
3-PLUS-1 ON KEY F1
READY.
10 VOL 8
20 FOR I=1 TO 14
30 READ X,Y
40 SOUND 1,X,Y
50 NEXT I
60 DATA 596,45,685,15,739,30,810,30
70 DATA 770,30,810,15,770,15,739,60
80 DATA 704,45,739,15,685,30,596,30
90 DATA 643,60,596,30
RUN
```

Note   The DATA command stores numbers that can be read in order using the command READ.

Piano

Make sure you are at the startup screen. Type in the following program, start it with
RUN, and press **RETURN**. To stop, press the **RUN STOP/ESC** key. The program is more
complicated, but it's also pretty cool.

```
10 SCNCLR
20 PRINT"USE KEYS 1..8 TO PLAY"
30 FOR X=1 TO 8
40 READ N(X)
50 NEXT X
60 VOL 8
80 GET A$
90 IF A$="" THEN GOTO 80
100 A=ASC(A$)
110 IF A<49 OR A>56 THEN GOTO 80
120 N=A-48
130 SOUND 1,N(N),5
140 COLOR 4,N,3
150 GOTO 80
160 DATA 169,262,345,383,453,516,571,596

READY.
RUN
```

Play *Twinkle Twinkle Little Star* with these keys: 1, 1, 5, 5, 6, 6, 5, 4, 4, 3, 3, 2, 2, 1, 5, 5,
4, 4, 3, 3, 2, 5, 5, 4, 4, 3, 3, 2, 1, 1, 5, 5, 6, 6, 5, 4, 4, 3, 3, 2, 2, 1.

Boxes

Make sure you are at the startup screen. Type in the following program, start it with **RUN**, and press **RETURN**.

```
10  COLOR 0,1
20  COLOR 1,2
30  GRAPHIC 1,1
40  A=RND(1)*20+10
50  FOR L=0 TO 359 STEP A
60  BOX 1,100,50,220,150,L
70  NEXT L
80  FOR L=1 TO 2000: NEXT L
90  GRAPHIC 0,1

READY.
RUN
```

Note   The RND command in line 40 gives a random number. So the screen will look different every time you run the program!

Circles

Make sure you are at the startup screen. If you previously typed in the Boxes program, all you need to do is type line 60. Otherwise, type in the following program, start it with **RUN**, and press **RETURN**.

```
10 COLOR 0,1
20 COLOR 1,2
30 GRAPHIC 1,1
40 A = RND(1)*20+10
50 FOR L=0 TO 359 STEP A
60 CIRCLE 1,160,100,80,40,,,L
70 NEXT L
80 FOR L=1 TO 2000:NEXT L
90 GRAPHIC 0,1

READY.
RUN
```

Note The RND command in line 40 gives a random number. So the screen will look different every time you run the program!

81

Blinking Graphics

Make sure you are at the startup screen. Type in the following program, start it with **RUN**, and press **RETURN**. To stop, press the **RUN STOP/ESC** key. The program is more complicated, but it's also pretty cool.

```
10 COLOR 0,1
20 GRAPHIC 3,1
30 COLOR 3,1
40 TRAP 200
50 DRAW 3,10,10 TO 10,100
51 DRAW 3,10,55 TO 30,55
60 DRAW 3,30,10 TO 30,100
61 DRAW 3,50,10 TO 80,10
70 DRAW 3,65,10 TO 65,100
71 DRAW 3,50,100 TO 80,100
80 FOR L=0 TO 7
90 COLOR 3,2,L
100 FOR M=1 TO 100: NEXT M
110 NEXT L
120 COLOR 3,1
130 FOR M=1 TO 100: NEXT M
140 GOTO 80
200 GRAPHIC 0: COLOR 1,1,7: COLOR 0,2

RUN
```

A Guessing Game

Make sure you are at the startup screen. Type in the following program, start it with **RUN**, and press **RETURN**. To stop, enter **0** as a guess.

```
10  G=0
20  M=INT(RND(1)*100)
30  PRINT"I AM THINKING OF A NUMBER."
40  PRINT"IT IS BETWEEN 1 AND 100."
50  PRINT"YOUR GUESS";
60  INPUT X
65  G=G+1
70  IF X=0 THEN END
80  IF X<M THEN PRINT "HIGHER":GOTO 50
90  IF X>M THEN PRINT "LOWER" :GOTO 50
100 PRINT"YES! YOU NEEDED";
110 PRINT G;
120 PRINT "GUESSES."

RUN
```

Summary

Have fun!

APPENDIX A

Saving and Loading

Once programs start to become larger and more complicated, you will not want to type them from scratch every time. You can save programs to permanent storage (for example, a tape, a disk, or, if you use an emulator, a hard disk). The internal setup and configuration of your permanent storage depends on the hardware or emulator choices you made as described in the preface. For example, VICE requires you to open an (empty) d64 file so a disk drive can be emulated (In the menu, select File ➤ Create and Attach Disk Image ➤ Unit #8 and then choose a file name ending with .d64).

Once you are set up, knowing the following commands comes in handy. The easiest way to store a program is using the command SAVE. The command takes a file name and a disk drive number as a parameter. The following screenshot shows a small program typed in followed by a SAVE command that is then executed by pressing RETURN.

```
COMMODORE BASIC V3.5 60671 BYTES FREE
3-PLUS-1 ON KEY F1

READY.
10 PRINT "HELLO WORLD"
20 GOTO 10

SAVE "HELLOWORLD",8

SAVING HELLOWORLD
READY.
```

© Gerald Friedland 2019
G. Friedland, *Beginning Programming Using Retro Computing*,
https://doi.org/10.1007/978-1-4842-4146-2

Since you do not see any error message on the screen, you can assume that the program has been saved. Let's restart the computer and load the program again. This is done by the LOAD command, which looks exactly like the SAVE command. The following screen shot shows the process followed by a LIST command, which shows that the program has indeed been loaded:

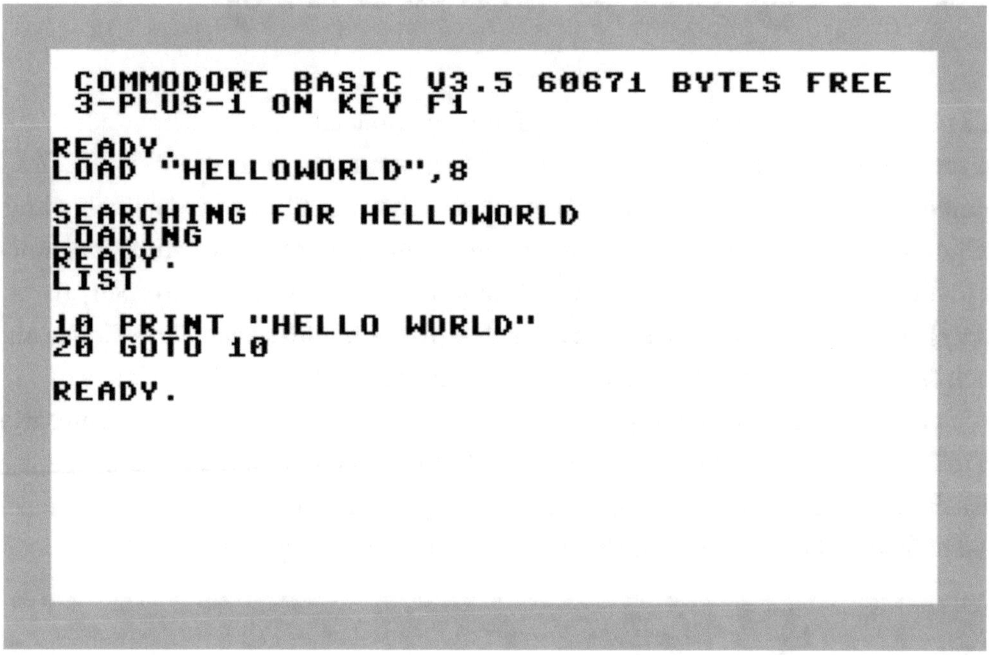

```
COMMODORE BASIC V3.5 60671 BYTES FREE
3-PLUS-1 ON KEY F1

READY.
LOAD "HELLOWORLD",8

SEARCHING FOR HELLOWORLD
LOADING
READY.
LIST

10 PRINT "HELLO WORLD"
20 GOTO 10

READY.
```

To get a listing of all programs on the disk, for example, to be reminded of the names of the available programs, type the command **LOAD "$", 8** followed by **LIST**. The following screen shot illustrates the way directories were listed in the 1980s (make sure you are at the start screen):

```
COMMODORE BASIC V3.5 60671 BYTES FREE
3-PLUS-1 ON KEY F1

READY.
LOAD"$",8

SEARCHING FOR $
LOADING
READY.
LIST

0 ▮▮▮▮▮▮▮▮▮▮▮▮▮▮▮▮▮▮▮▮▮▮    "    26]
1      "HELLOWORLD"          PRG
663 BLOCKS FREE.

READY.
■
```

Caution   When you load a directory, your current program is erased. So don't load the directory in an attempt to find out under which name you want to save your program. Also, tape recorders do not have a directory listing. Trying to load the directory form tape is a giant waste of time.

Summary

Loading and saving programs both require the configuration of the emulator or underlying hardware. On the original Commodore hardware, loading and saving from a cassette tape was worth it only for more than about 30 lines of code.

Index

© Gerald Friedland 2019
G. Friedland, *Beginning Programming Using Retro Computing,*
https://doi.org/10.1007/978-1-4842-4146-2

Printed in the United States
By Bookmasters